The Wisdom Deck Book

**A BUDDHIST GUIDE TO PLAYING
THE CARDS YOU'RE DEALT WITHOUT
GETTING LOST IN THE SHUFFLE**

Elizabeth Gosselin

Yoga of Compassion

San Anselmo, CA

Text © 2017 by Elizabeth Gosselin
Illustration © 2015 by Heidi Kalyana

Library of Congress Cataloging-in-Publication Data
Gosselin, Elizabeth.

The Wisdom Deck – A Buddhist Guide for
Playing The Hand You're Dealt
Without Getting Lost in the Shuffle

Includes index.
ISBN: 978-0-9985150-0–7 (hardbound)
ISBN: 978-0-9985150-1-4 (softbound)
ISBN: 978-0-9985150-2-1 (e-book)

Yoga of Compassion, Publisher
San Anselmo, CA
415/455-9872

www.thewisdomdeck.com

Copy Editor: Anne Cushman
Design: *the*BookDesigners

For Andy,
Giving me the courage to be
fearless and to share what I know.

Contents

A Special Note to Readers

The original format of this body of work is in a 'Card Deck' format. I felt it would be beneficial for readers to have this material in a book format for easy-to-use portable reference. This soft cover book contains the same material as the 52-card deck. What you are now are holding in your hands is the book format of *The Wisdom Deck ~ A Buddhist Guide for Playing the Cards You're Dealt Without Getting Lost in the Shuffle!*

The *Wisdom Deck Book* is available for purchase through independent booksellers and Amazon. Yoga of Compassion also occasionally distributes this book without charge to persons interested in learning more about the practice of meditation and/or are interested in Buddhist teachings and who may not have the resources to purchase it.

If you have received a book for free or would like to make this book available to anyone regardless of financial ability, please consider making a donation to Yoga of Compassion. Your donation will go to the costs of future publications and will be freely distributed to people who may not be able to purchase this valuable resource.

If you are part of an organization that serves marginalized groups including the homeless, minorities, youth at risk, the disabled, prisoners, the elderly, and those without access to education and believe they would benefit from these teachings please contact me about making *The Wisdom Deck Book* available to the individuals who you serve.

Yoga of Compassion will also donate a portion of the proceeds from this book to the scholarships funds of meditation centers that offer retreats. These donations are intended to help offset the costs for individuals who need assistance to be able to participate in a retreat.

~Elizabeth

Start where you are.

The Wisdom Deck Book

A BUDDHIST GUIDE FOR PLAYING THE CARDS YOU'RE DEALT WITHOUT GETTING LOST IN THE SHUFFLE

My inspiration

I created the Wisdom Deck using summaries of talks I gave over a three-year period of time when I led meditation study groups. In Theravada Buddhism these meditation groups are referred to as Kalyana Mitta or 'spiritual friends.' These groups share the common values of a silent meditation practice and exploring the wisdom teachings that support, develop and enliven daily life.

These concise summaries can aid students in several ways. First, they can be a reminder of the rituals of a meditation practice. Second, they may be used to help develop a better understanding of spiritual themes. Lastly, they can be a quick reference and study guide for Buddhist teachings and terms. As I developed these summaries on handheld cards and began to give them away to my students and spiritual friends, I found that they received much joy and gratification from using them.

The cards evolved into the Wisdom Deck -- a way to 'play,' study and connect with the teachings and insights of a spiritual practice. These concise teachings are a support to help navigate through the tough times in our lives when we face loss and illness, depression and grief, fear and anxiety. They are meant to help us face these life challenges and find inspiration to heal, transform and embody spiritual truths. They also provide clarity, insight and encouragement so that we can be calm and clear without getting lost in the shuffle of our daily dramas.

Outlined below you will find various creative ways to use these teachings. Some are direct teachings for formal practice used by monastic and lay practitioners alike. Others are my own renditions and interpretations of teachings passed down to me from my teachers. I am not a Buddhist scholar by any stretch of the imagination. However, like many lay practitioners, I have found great refuge as a dedicated spiritual practitioner exploring the wisdom teachings of the Buddha and the many traditions of Eastern spiritual practices.

General Instructions for Meditation

In my experience as a meditator I have found it is always best to find a knowledgeable and respected teacher. While there are many good books, CDs, DVDs, YouTube videos and podcasts on how to meditate, it is also enormously helpful, almost imperative, to attend a meditation group meeting, a day-long or even a week-long meditation retreat and receive live instruction among like-minded individuals with an experienced teacher. Remember, there is no experience necessary when it comes to beginning a spiritual or meditation practice. In the words of renowned meditation teacher, Pema Chodron, "start where you are."

What are the Wisdom Teachings?

These teachings are powerful tools – they contain rituals, practices, prayers and mantras that you can use in your daily life and meditation practice. Some are short synopses of important Buddhist teachings that can be used as a reminder or a 'flash card' to touch into particular qualities or practices that we explore as students of the dharma. Others are precursors to the practice of meditation that prepare the mind and steady our attention. Some are skillful ways to end a meditation session.

The Wisdom Teachings presented here are also compact reminders for training the mind. As with any form of learning or discipline, over time we gradually develop and build a solid foundation and understanding. Through stabilizing the mind, we can apply our new knowledge to respond to life in more beneficial ways. For example, we can begin to see opportunities in the small disappointments and frustrations of everyday life and respond with wisdom and compassion.

Using these teachings takes our mindset and shapes it into an open and accepting way of living. We each have an inner inclination towards happiness and peace. Using these practices allows us to create beautiful, beneficial and wholesome qualities reinforcing our intention to live happy and joyful lives and contribute to the joy and well-being of others.

How to Work With These Themes

You may use any of these themes in a regular sitting practice, as a way to guide your day, or in any way that supports your spiritual life. You can say or recite their teachings silently to yourself or you may choose to speak them out loud using different tones of voice. You may even chant or sing them as Buddhist communities often do when they gather together for several hours or on a long retreat. You may notice that some lend themselves more easily to chanting or singing than others.

One way to use a theme is to pick one from a section. For example choose one of **The Paramis, The Seven Factors of Awakening or Practices for Opening the Mind and Heart** -- and work with this particular theme or teaching for a week or a month, coming back to it again and again and noticing your reflections and responses over a period of time.

If you would like to explore deeper into a practice you might read the teaching and then relate your response to the first three Foundations of **Mindfulness—Mindfulness of Body, Mindfulness of Feeling Tone and Mindfulness of Mind.**

- When reading about this particular subject, what do you notice in your body? Bring your awareness to the *body.* Notice temperature, breath, heaviness or other senses.

- What do you notice about the *feeling tone* (vedana)? Do you have an aversion to a particular theme or do you feel neutral? Does one theme seem easy to understand and another difficult, annoying or confusing?

- What does the *mind* do? Where does it go? Do you find yourself more interested in certain themes? Do you have an aversion towards others? Are there some you do not quite understand?

Remember there is nothing to do or fix. This is simply an inquiry into themes and ideas contained within the teachings of Buddhism. This is an opportunity to discover how they might resonate or catch you in a particular way. Recognize how you respond and take note of how your response relates to your personal experience. Use this internal feedback as an opportunity to investigate and reflect on how you relate to wholesome ideas.

As you work with the themes in ways you feel most comfortable, you may begin to feel a shifting of intention as you go about your daily life. Slowly over time you may begin to find yourself aligning with wholesome values and sensing a new way of being. You may find these qualities bring a sense of strength and an open-heartedness for yourself that flows to all sentient beings you come in contact with. They may even change how you see and participate in the world.

Remember there is no one right way to use these teachings. Any one of the approaches mentioned here and the unique ways you find to use them on your own will lead you towards a greater knowing and understanding of all the rest.

Description

Beginnings and Endings

Beginnings and Endings are the 'bookends' of a formal mediation practice. They are what allow us to 'settle in' and prepare the mind and body to begin the exploration of mindful awareness. They build a foundation for stability and set an intention for practice. Other cards in this section are classic ways Buddhist meditators honor the tradition or practice. At the beginning of a long period of meditation or silent retreat, practitioners typically chant the precepts as a way to signify their dedication and commitment to a time of spiritual devotion. At the end of the practice they 'dedicate the merit' or the benefit the practice has brought to all living beings so that they may live with ease and peace.

The Four Foundations of Mindfulness:
The Sattipatthana Sutta

The Four Foundations of Mindfulness are the Buddha's instructions on the four ways to establish and understand mindfulness. These instructions are explicit ways to aid in understanding the mind and body interconnectedness and how to work towards freeing the mind from the causes of suffering. The complete sutta contains all of the Buddha's teachings.

For purposes of this body of work I have included the first three foundations of Mindfulness: *Mindfulness of the Body, Mindfulness of Feeling Tones (Vedana),* and *Mindfulness of Mind.* The forth Foundation of the Sattihatthana Sutta is Mindfulness of Dhammas and from this foundation I have included *The Four Noble Truths, The Eightfold Path, The Two Truths* and *The Seven Factors of Awakening.*

Mindfulness of Dhammas traditionally includes additional teachings on: *The Five Hindrances, The Five Aggregates of Clinging* and *The Six Sense Spheres.* I have not included these three instructional teachings in this book, as they are more advanced practices to be explored in a future deck.

The Four Radiant States of Mind:
The Brahma Viharas

The four Brahma Viharas represent the most beautiful and hopeful aspects of our true human nature. They are mindfulness practices that protect the mind from falling into unwholesome habitual patterns of reactiveness.

The Brahma Viharas are also referred to as the *four immeasurables* and *mind liberating practices*, as they awaken powerful healing energies which brighten and lift the mind to increasing levels of clarity. As a result, these boundless states of loving-kindness, compassion, sympathetic joy and equanimity manifest as forces of purification that transform the turbulent heart into a refuge of calm, focused awareness.

The phrases found in the Brahma Viharas and on many other cards are affirmational. These are powerful resolves that have the ability to shape our heart and mind. When we use the frame 'may I' we put our heart upon a focus or intention. With intention we set a direction for the highest aspiration for ourselves. We give impetus to the resolve and move towards deeper clarity in the heart and mind.

The Three Characteristics of Existence

The Three Characteristics of Existence are a simple form of the Buddha's teaching found in the Four Noble Truths. The first truth is impermanence (anicca), the second is not-self (anatta), and the third is unsatisfactoriness or suffering (dukkha). These three characteristics are apparent in all conditioned phenomena. Therefore, every sensation, thought and experience we have is subject to these three characteristics.

The Paramis: The Ten Perfections

The Paramis or 'perfections' support the Seven Factors of Awakening. They provide the practitioner with worthy and wholesome intentions. As we continue to incline the mind toward these wholesome qualities in our thoughts, actions and speech we begin to abandon unskillful actions. The Paramis are like the spokes of a wheel, one doesn't necessarily precede or follow the next, rather, they are all connected and support one another in our efforts.

The Seven Factors of Awakening: Bojjhanga

The Seven Factors of Awakening encompass many of the spiritual qualities frequently mentioned by the Buddha as extraordinarily beneficial for spiritual development. The factors, sometimes referred to as *treasures*, are transpersonal as they move beyond habitual identity, moods and reactions.

The Seven Factors of Awakening are accessible to all of us, but they must be *developed* and *refined*. Developing these factors together deepens and supports the other, as they are dependent on one another. When the Seven Factors are continually cultivated, they contribute to greater knowledge and wisdom and eventually bring liberation.

You will notice that both Energy (Viriya) and Equanimity (Upekkha) are contained in both the Seven Factors and the Paramis. The repetition of these two qualities emphasizes how important they are to the Buddhist practice!

Practices for Opening the Heart and Mind

The practices for Opening the Heart and Mind are a compilation of themes I have found valuable in my own spiritual practice. Some of the teachings included here are drawn from traditional Buddhist practices and others are not. Self-Compassion, Gratitude and Humility do not appear in traditional teaching lists as qualities or virtues to align with or develop. However, I feel they have been implied throughout the suttas. My mentoring teachers have taught these themes and practices and I have either simply shared their direct teachings or created my own interpretation.

You will also notice that this section draws from different Buddhist traditions. I have found this to be very useful in my personal practice. There is a deep reservoir of cross-denominational Buddhist wisdom teachings that can support, develop, and expand a spiritual practice more fully. I invite you to explore this section with curiosity and interest.

Awareness of Death

Meditation on the Awareness of Death is of one of the oldest practices in all Buddhist traditions. In Western cultures we rarely contemplate death and therefore are wholly unprepared when someone we love passes away or when we are facing our own death. When we consciously bring a greater awareness of our inevitable death and the death of those who we love, we relieve ourselves of a natural source of anxiety, conscious or unconscious. Awareness of death helps to acknowledge the impermanent nature of everything and it deepens our understanding of what it means to be alive.

The Wisdom Deck Book

**A BUDDHIST GUIDE FOR
PLAYING THE CARDS YOU'RE DEALT
WITHOUT GETTING LOST IN THE SHUFFLE**

Beginnings and Endings

Invocation

I now open to the infinite grace and
wisdom that resides deep within me.

I take this time to acknowledge the spiritual masters
and teachers who have come before me and brought
me to this place. May the essence of these
enlightened beings be invoked within me now.

I give thanks for the teachings and insights
that have been passed down through the ages.
May these insights calm my mind
and open my heart.

May I be awakened and be free
so that I may help all beings realize happiness
and be free from suffering.

Intention

CENTANA

My intention for my meditation practice today is to calm my mind, relax my body and open to love for myself and others and to find kindness, compassion and equanimity in all things.

May I open my mind and contemplate the true nature of reality as a remedy to unhappiness and dissatisfaction.

I dedicate my practice to the community (sangha) of humanity.

May the teachings and wisdom of the dharma bring greater awareness and freedom as I aim towards enlightenment (nibbana).

May I contribute to the well being of all people everywhere.

Taking Refuge
TISARANA~THE THREE JEWELS

I take refuge in the Buddha,
I trust and open to my own basic goodness
and its opening into a life of freedom.

I take refuge in the dharma, *the wisdom teachings*
of kindness, compassion and generosity.

I take refuge in the sangha,
this community of practitioners
and awakening spiritual beings.

I realize there is nothing to join,
and nothing to become. I am simply opening my heart
to a sacred connection with this world.

Chant
Buddham saranam gacchami
Dhammam saranam gacchami
Sangham saranam gacchami

Dutiyampi saranam gacchami
Dutiyampi saranam gacchami
Dutiyampi saranam gacchami

Tyatiyampi buddham saranam gacchami
Tyatiyampi dhammam saranam gacchami
Tyatiyampi sangham saranam gacchami

Taking the Five Precepts

PANACA-SILANI

I vow to do no harm to any living being

I vow not to take what is not given freely

I vow to abstain from sexual misconduct

I vow to abstain from false or harmful speech

*I vow to refrain from ingesting intoxicants that
would in any way cloud my mind*

Bodhisattva Vow

May I be a guard for those who need protection.
A guide for those on the path.
A boat, a raft, a bridge for those
who wish to cross the flood.
May I be a lamp in the darkness.
A resting place for the weary.
A healing medicine for all who are sick.
A voice of plenty, a tree of miracles.
And for the boundless multitudes of living beings,
may I bring sustenance and awakening.
Enduring like earth and sky,
until all beings are freed from sorrow
and all are awakened.

BY: SHANTIDEVA AS TRANSLATED BY THE DALAI LAMA

Mindfulness of Breath
ANAPANASATI

First settle the body by becoming aware of the body.
Consciously relax and let go of knots,
tension, pain or places in the body
where there may be holding or feelings of constriction.

Find comfort or gentle awareness or simple
acceptance of the body as it is right now
without judgment or criticism.

Bring attention to the breath.
Notice the sensation of breath
whether it be cool or warm
as it flows in and out of the nostrils.
Or bring awareness to the
expansion and deflation of the chest.
Or bring awareness to the belly expanding, relaxing.

Stay with a focused awareness to the breath.
No need to change the breath in any way.
Observe the breath.

Be with the breath.
Come back to the breath again and again.

Mindfulness of Breathing

Breathing in, I know I am breathing in
Breathing out, I know I am breathing out
Breathing in a long breath, I know I am breathing in a long breath
Breathing out a long breath, I know I am breathing out a long breath
Breathing in a short breath, I know I am breathing in a short breath
Breathing out a short breath,
I know I am breathing out a short breath

Breathing in, I am aware of my whole body
Breathing out, I am aware of my whole body
Breathing in, I feel joyful. Breathing out, I feel joyful
Breathing in, I feel happy. Breathing out, I feel happy

Breathing in, I am aware of my mental formations
Breathing out, I am aware of my mental formations
Breathing in, I calm my mental formations
Breathing out, I calm my mental formations

Breathing in, I am aware of my mind
Breathing out, I am aware of my mind
Breathing in, I make my mind happy
Breathing out, I make my mind happy

Breathing in, I concentrate my mind
Breathing out, I concentrate my mind
Breathing in, I liberate my mind
Breathing out, I liberate my mind

Breathing in, I observe the impermanent nature of all dharmas
Breathing out, I observe the impermanent nature of all dharmas
Breathing in, I observe the disappearance of desire
Breathing out, I observe the disappearance of desire
Breathing in, I observe cessation. Breathing out, I observe cessation
Breathing in, I observe letting go. Breathing out, I observe letting go

—THICH NHAT HAHN

Dedication of Merit
CLOSING

May whatever goodness this practice
generated be of benefit to all people
everywhere regardless of race, color,
religion, class, gender, or sexual orientation.

May all those who are subject to aggression,
violence and prejudice, experience equanimity.
May all those who are suffering from grief,
sorrow and pain be relieved and find freedom.

May our hearts and minds unify
through goodness and generosity.
May we all call forth our own inner
compassion and wisdom.

May we all awaken to greater happiness and joy.
May all living beings come together to share
in illumination and peace.

The Four Foundations of Mindfulness

The Sattipatthana Sutta

Mindfulness of the Body

This body is a temporary vessel through which
we experience the activities of the body and mind.
The body is made up of anatomical parts and elements
that combine into physical form to carry us on this journey.
It is our work to become acutely aware of the parts
and elements of the physical body.
Through this awareness combined with breath,
we connect the body with our heart and mind.

Our task is to study the components of our human form
and become acquainted with them intimately
and at the same time recognize their inherent impermanence.
They will change, break down, die and decay.
We contemplate, embrace and marvel
at the changing nature of this human body,
as a temporary vessel that allows for
an intimate understanding of life and death.

As we bring greater awareness to the body and breath
we awaken to a deeper knowing and a felt sense of
what is happening in the mind.
Through this mind-body awareness we build
a greater capacity to observe thoughts as they arise and
see the true nature of mind as ever changing.
When we ground or anchor our experience of the present moment
through mindfulness of the body we protect against
distraction, attachment and clinging.

Mindfulness of Feeling Tone
VEDANA

Vedana is the Pali term used to describe a 'feeling tone'
that arises when we come into contact with sense objects.
It results when our senses meet a sense object and we experience it as
attractive, neutral or unattractive.
For example, when we experience vedana through our eyes
we may see a beautiful flower and be attracted. This is pleasant vedana.

There is also unpleasant and neutral vedana, through which desire,
grasping and becoming are stimulated. We want to possess what we desire.
This is true for all our senses and the objects they come in contact with –
sight, sound, smell, taste, touch and thought.
Some of our thoughts are pleasant, some are neither pleasant nor unpleasant,
and some are unpleasant.

Through our practice we open to omnipresent sensitivity and
all the possibilities for pain, ugliness and unpleasantness.

Through mindfulness of vedana we begin to notice a desire arise
when seeing something beautiful and wanting it or
seeing something ugly and desiring to get rid of it.
This is the natural reaction on the sensory plane.
As we develop a reflective mind we can contemplate vedana
through our sensory organs and recognize 'this is the way it is,'
there is nothing wrong, in fact it is okay.
Our response changes and we recognize there is
pleasant, painful, and neutral.
We practice to accept things as they are rather
than reacting and moving towards or away.

Vedana is not to be confused with **emotional** *feelings.*

Mindfulness of Mind

In mindfulness of mind we first develop awareness of
the three unwholesome states of mind.
They are greed and lust, hatred and anger,
ignorance and delusion (bewilderment and confusion).
In addition to recognizing these unwholesome states of mind
and when they are present,
it is equally important to notice when they are absent.
It is when they are absent that we experience a wholesome state of mind.

Through mindfulness we cultivate the ability to remain receptively aware
of these wholesome and unwholesome states so that the mind can
remain free and unattached from them as they arise and pass away.

After recognizing wholesome and unwholesome states of mind
we then become mindful of both the contraction of mind in sloth and
the distraction of mind in restlessness.
As we develop this capacity we no longer get lost in
or become identified with either of these states.
The mind then finds the balance necessary for deeper concentration
and higher states of mind that follow.

Being mindful of all these states when they arise is the path to freedom.
Through bare attention and mirror-like wisdom,
we see their ephemeral, impermanent, and selfless nature.
Simply noticing the general quality of the mind as it is influenced
by different mind states, moods or emotions is sufficient for liberation.
A liberated mind experiences mental freedom, calm and insight.

ADAPTED FROM: "MINDFULNESS: A PRACTICAL GUIDE
TO AWAKENING" BY JOSEPH GOLDSTEIN

The Four Noble Truths

CHATTARI-ARIYA-SACCANI

Life contains moments of suffering (dukkha).

The cause of suffering is clinging or craving
to desired objects and states of being.

Suffering is released by letting go of
clinging to these desires or cravings.

There is an Eightfold Path
to freedom from suffering.

The Four Noble Truths are the practices of insight and
realization in and of itself. The Four Noble Truths
are a teaching of how to live wisely.

—PHILLIP MOFFITT

The Noble Eight-Fold Path
ARIYA ATTHANGIKA MAGGA

The path that leads to the end of suffering

Wise Understanding
Seeing and understanding things as they really are—
impermanent and imperfect.

Wise Intention
Resisting craving and desire and the drive for gratification.
Committing to ethical actions of kindness and good will. An intention
of not harming and showing compassion in body, mind and speech.

Wise Speech
Abstaining from false, slanderous, harsh, sarcastic speech
and idle chatter that lacks purpose. Telling the truth in a warm
and friendly manner and speaking only when appropriate.

Wise Action
Refraining from harming others or taking what is not given freely.
Being respectful and safe regarding sexual relationships.
Acting kindly, compassionately and honestly.

Wise Livelihood
Choosing actions and a vocation that are in tune with
increasing what is good and helpful and decreasing harmfulness.

Wise Effort
An energetic determination to let go of unwholesome states of mind
and to cultivate wholesome, positive states of mind.

Wise Mindfulness
Cultivating a mind that is present, open, quiet, and alert to this moment.
An awareness of an ability to actively observe thoughts
and choose intention.

Wise Concentration
Developing wholesome consciousness and a state where
mental faculties are unified and directed and the mind stable and clear.
Concentration is strengthened through meditation practice.

The Two Truths

RELATIVE AND ULTIMATE

Whatever is dependently co-arisen
That is explained to be emptiness.
That, being a dependent designation
Is itself the middle way.

Something that is not dependently arisen,
Such a thing does not exist.
Therefore a non-empty thing
Does not exist.

—Nagarjuna Verses 24:18 & 19

Knowledge of the relative and ultimate truths provides insight
into the interrelated ways of understanding emptiness.

Relative truth is the conventional way of identifying subject and object
and how they work. This understanding directs our worldly activities.
While objects appear to exist as separate things, this sensory-cognitive
appearance is illusory.

While relative truth explains emptiness as dependent arising, ultimate
truth demonstrates the emptiness of phenomena. The union of relative
and ultimate truths inform and express the other.

For example: to see deception is to be free of deception, like a magician
who knows the magic trick. When one is no longer fooled by false
appearances, phenomena are neither reified nor denied.

Ultimate truth is the understanding of emptiness, that all phenomena
are empty of an inherent nature or essence. Phenomenon is not a thing,
rather a sequence of arising and ceasing from moment to moment or
conditioned arising.

When we are no longer ruled by the attraction and aversion that
accompanies the reification of phenomena, equanimity becomes possible.

Awakening to the two truths is going beyond both
appearance and emptiness.

The Four Radiant States of Mind

The Brahma Viharas

Loving Kindness

METTA

Neutralizes negativity, self-doubt, resentment or hatred

For you:
May I be filled with love and kindness
May I be safe and protected from inner and outer harm
May I be healthy and well in body and mind
May I be free from suffering and
be filled with joy and happiness

For someone you love or who has benefited you:
May you be filled with love and kindness
May you be safe from inner and outer harm
May you be well and at ease in body and mind
May you be joyful and happy

For a neutral person:
May you be filled with love and kindness
May you be safe and protected from inner and outer harm
May you be healthy and well in body and mind
May you be free from suffering and
be filled with joy and happiness

For someone with whom you have difficulty:
May you be filled with love and kindness
May you be safe and protected from inner and outer harm
May you be well and at ease in body and mind
May you be joyful and happy

Compassion
KARUNA

Counters the afflictive thoughts of hostility and harm

Just like me, this person wants to be happy
Just like me, this person has known pain and suffering
Just like me, this person is doing the best that they can
Just like me, this person wants to love and to be loved

May I be free from suffering.
May you be free from suffering.
May I be held in kindness just as I am.
May you be held in kindness just as you are.
May we be at ease in our bodies, hearts and minds.

Sympathetic Joy

MUDITA

Counters the feelings of envy and jealousy

I rejoice in your happiness.

I take delight in your health and good fortune.

I celebrate your happiness.

May your happiness continue to expand.

May your happiness and good fortune never cease.

May the happiness and good fortune of all beings
increase further and further.

I know there is enough happiness for all.
Happiness is unlimited and omnipresent.

Equanimity

UPEKKHA

Neutralizes Anxiety and Restlessness

May I recognize and release any unseen
biases I may have and cultivate an equitable
attitude towards all beings.

May I learn to act from even-mindedness
and open-heartedness.

May I cultivate an unbiased attitude towards all beings and
recognize that friends, enemies and strangers
are my community of humanity, we are interbeings.

May I be awakened to appreciate each person and
recognize their right to happiness.

May my mind be free from feelings of
attachment, aversion and indifference.

May I be balanced, open and peaceful.

May I be present in each moment to see the
arising and passing of each emotion and
mental tendency with calm abiding.

From this basis of equilibrium, may I be free to
cultivate love, compassion and an open heart
for the benefit of all beings everywhere.

The Three Characteristics of Existence

Impermanence

ANICCA

One of the Three Characteristics of Existence

The body is an infinite collection of living cells moving,
multiplying, and dying.
The mind is thoughts, perceptions, feelings never ceasing,
ever changing, a flow of mental experience.
Things that surround you, the seat, the room, and objects are
a mass of particles that only appear solid and static.

Everything is impermanent.

Beyond the city, the country: its trees, hills, mountains, forests
and deserts are all changing, growing, transforming and ceasing.
Oceans, rivers, streams are all moving, flowing, changing course,
direction and substance.
People, animals, insects all grow, change, die.

The earth, the universe and galaxies beyond are forever evolving,
expanding, disintegrating, and disappearing.

Cultivate a clear, strong feeling of the ever-changing nature of all
things. Bring stillness to the mind, contemplate the
impermanence of all people, places, things, even this life.
Rouse thoughts and insights that it is unrealistic to cling
to things as if they were permanent.
Nothing is permanent.

Whatever is beautiful and pleasing will change and
eventually disappear. In the same way, whatever is unpleasant or
disturbing is not forever. It will change too. There is no lasting
happiness by grasping to things that change. Allow the mind
to expand and develop an acceptance of Impermanence.

Not Self

ANATTA

One of the Three Characteristics of Existence

When I can let go of me or mine . . .
When I no longer have to identify with
a particular role or identity . . .

When my ego no longer forces its way through
to prove to myself . . .

When I give up my view or an opinion . . .

When I no longer crave to be seen or heard,
recognized or acknowledged . . .

When I am no longer attached to having things my way . . .

When I give up being right or wrong or striving
to accomplish something . . .

When I earnestly take appropriate action
and let go of the outcome . . .

When I stop objecting to how things are . . .
When I no longer wish for things to be different . . .

When I learn to just be . . . Still

Then, *and only then*, can I rest in peaceful, mindful
awareness without grasping or clinging.
I can be free.

Suffering

DUKKHA

One of the Three Characteristics of Existence

I am aware of my own suffering and the suffering of
others. I recognize that I am not immune from:

Physical and mental pain.
The constant changing nature of my life and this world.
The inherent unsatisfactoriness of life itself.

I accept this truth as the nature of being alive.
Through this acceptance I work towards being with
the suffering of all living beings and
the universal suffering of this world.

May this insight provide me the wisdom in the truth
that Life is Like This.

With this knowledge and wisdom, may I find freedom
in this truth. May I now open to the possibility that I
might lessen my own pain and the pain of others,
through following a path of
greater insight and meaning.

The Paramis

The Ten Perfections

Generosity

DANA

Generosity is an open heartfelt response to life,
an aspiration to grow beyond the narrow
confines of our own small world.

Generosity is not necessarily about giving material
'things,' it is about giving appreciation and love to
one another. We give love and appreciation through
hospitality, kind and affectionate speech,
listening with attention.

Generosity is a simple, natural and spontaneous
response of *internal* wealth and abundance.

Generosity is a creative expression of positive
mental states, taking form in the world
as a constant flow of generous
thoughts, words and actions.

———

I am aware that true giving has no giver, no gift, and
no receiver. As I practice generosity, I let go of
self as the benefactor, the value of the gift,
or acknowledgment by the receiver.
This view supports the pure act of giving.

As I cultivate non-attachment to material and
immaterial 'things' as they are, I establish inner
contentment and I open myself to the needs of
others through generosity.

Ethical Conduct

SILA

Ethics are guidelines for living. Sometimes called virtues
or moral conduct they contribute to
self-discipline and help steer our
thoughts, actions and speech.

Ethical conduct is a commitment to
social justice, equality and contributing to
the healing of our world.

These standards lend clarity and power to our lives.
They allow us freedom from unwholesome distractions and the
opportunity to live positively, to grow spiritually, and
to naturally help others along the way.

In practicing sila we refrain from unwise actions by
doing good deeds, being generous and giving selfless
service to benefit other beings.

———

I practice doing no harm and seek to do only good
and to support, cherish and protect life.

I practice not taking what is not offered freely, living
more simply, less selfishly and with greater awareness
of the welfare of others.

I practice abstaining from false or harmful speech and
aim for honesty, truthfulness and kindness.

I practice abstaining from sexual misconduct and
show respect for my partner, others, and myself in
healthy sexual expressions.

I practice refraining from ingesting intoxicants and
commit to living an awake, aware and responsible life.

Renunciation

NEKKHAMMA

Happiness is not attained through
having, acquiring or storing something.
As we develop the strength of clarity to see
that things and experiences do not lead to
ultimate happiness, we find peace
in moment-to-moment awareness.

Renunciation is letting go of the
gratification of getting what we want,
and the mental habit of wanting itself.

Renunciation asks us to look at
habits that limit and enslave us.

Renunciation allows us to see craving for what it is,
and gives us the wisdom to relinquish its hold on us.

———

I recognize that what I have is adequate.
It is enough. When I reach for more
I lose my perspective and my balance.

I let go of my attachments to status, beliefs,
opinions and assumptions as to who I am.

I cultivate contentment and inner strength to
be with things as they are, rather than focus
on the way it is *not*.

I'm enough! Right now, always and
in every moment.

Wisdom
PANNA

Wisdom is a quality or state of being
that embodies wise knowing of what is true or natural
coupled with discernment and insight.

Wisdom is putting aside both the desire
to increase pleasant experiences,
and the urge to resist unpleasant experiences.

Wisdom is deep understanding or clarity, rather
than a learned storehouse of knowledge.

Through meditation, we have the opportunity
to know the mind and look beneath the
mirage of its activity and then restrain
the worry, impatience and conceit.

———

I understand my actions (kamma) have consequences,
therefore I act with wise intention.

When I move beyond my innate opinions,
reactions and biases, and respond with
open-hearted kindness, I am practicing wisdom.

When I understand the nature of my mind,
delusion changes into wisdom.

In practicing wisdom, I remove the fuel of neediness
and craving, and wise knowing becomes available to me.

When I yoke wisdom with compassion
I find ultimate and supreme wisdom.

Energy
VIRIYA

Energy is interest, curiosity and exploration.

What we attend to, we energize;
what is energized, governs our world.

Energy, when applied to calm insight,
can free the mind from stress and suffering.

Energy is making a balanced effort to sustain wise
endeavors rather than using brute force.

May I use my energy and best efforts to
investigate my true nature,
and eliminate doubt and worry.

In reflecting on the best use of my energy I ask,
"Do my intentions and actions benefit my
welfare and the welfare of others? Do they
lead away from stress and towards peace?"

With mindful awareness, I channel my energy
towards that which is supportive and nourishing.

My energy comes from the strength and the
courage to have an open heart.

Patience
KHANTI

Patience is not mindlessly enduring; it is the gentle application
of steady perseverance.

Patience comes from inner strength and consistency.
When we hold difficult times as opportunities
we can build capacity for deep patience.

Patience has the qualities of forgiveness, understanding and trust.
It opens our hearts to the suffering heart of another.

Patience has a character of acceptance. The activity of patience
is to meet and be with the desirable and undesirable.
Patience is taking wise action in what we value,
it is not resignation or fear or collapse or giving up.

Patience is firm and steady in the face of uncertainty or
undesirable situations. When we have patience we do not shrink
or in defeat struggle or fight, for opposition is delusion.

———

When I let go of having or wanting things a particular way,
I find the freedom of practicing patience and trusting life.

I find my inner patient self when I notice an impulse to react
and instead I relax into acceptance and kindness.

I accept what is happening right now and refrain from unskillful acts.
I maintain steady perseverance despite what I perceive as difficulty.

Loving-Kindness

METTA

Loving-kindness is an unconditional,
inclusive love imbued with wisdom.

It is only after we practice with deep care
and compassion for ourselves,
breaking down any resistance or
barriers to our own attitudes of self worth,
that we can then extend loving-kindness to others.
We then extend loving-kindness to those we easily love,
those we are neutral towards and
those with whom we have difficulty.

Every living being has the potential to love without reservation.
Every living being deserves to be loved unconditionally.

Loving-kindness is a meditation of care, concern,
and tenderness for oneself and for all people.

When we practice loving-kindness,
both during formal meditation practice
and in everyday life, we are practicing softening
the heart and mind and opening to deeper levels
of a sense of kindness, of pure unbiased love.

Loving-kindness is not a desire to possess another or to be
sentimental. Love and friendship is not an obligation. Instead,
loving-kindness comes from a selfless place without the
expectation to receive anything in return.

Honesty

SACCA

Honesty asks us to look at the nature of our thoughts,
attitudes and biases through introspection and meditation.

It is the ability to see or
know things in an undistorted way.

When we have integrity and act honestly,
we are being true to our word.
When we are honest we build trust in ourselves
knowing we have purpose and an ability to
contribute in meaningful ways.

Honesty provides a good conscience
and is both a pleasure and a relief.
Honesty is a powerful antidote to strain and stress.

Honesty doesn't need to be strident or blunt.
It can be subtle, considered and refined.

Honesty is the intention just before speaking to
refrain from telling lies, reporting rumors or gossiping.

———

Before speaking I ask myself: Is what I am
about to say true, kind, or necessary?
Then I ask: Is this the right moment to speak up?

When I am straightforward and honest, I find my
inner truth and quiet strength.

Resolve

ADHITTHANA

Resolve is an inner determination
and the ability to have a strong and clear intention.

When we set our mind to directing our actions towards
wholesome qualities of the heart and mind, we practice resolve.

We strengthen the power of resolve when we
recognize that we are 'off course' and we come
back into alignment with our aspiration.

Resolve is moving through the difficulties and
challenges that life brings
with wholesome aspiration and motivation.

Having resolve is not about accomplishing or succeeding.
It is not about failure or defeat. Resolve is a living and
dynamic quality, it is the heart responding
to life with strength and clarity.

———

When I encounter laziness or inertia, I find the
energy to recommit myself to practicing awareness.

My intention is to cultivate generosity and to train in peace.

Just for today, I resolve to act from a natural
sense of love and compassion.

Equanimity

UPEKKHA

May I learn to act from even-mindedness
and open-heartedness.

May I cultivate an unbiased attitude towards all beings and
recognize that friends, enemies and strangers
are my community of humanity,
we are interbeings.

May I be awakened to appreciate each person and
recognize their right to happiness.

May my mind be free from feelings of
attachment, aversion and indifference.

May I be balanced, open and peaceful.

May I be present in each moment to see the
arising and passing of each emotion and
mental tendency with calm abiding.

From this basis of equilibrium, may I be free to cultivate
love, compassion and an open heart
for the benefit of all beings everywhere.

The Seven Factors of Awakening

Bojjhanga

Mindfulness

SATI

Being mindful is an antidote to aversion

Mindfulness is being aware and receptive in the
present moment without judgment. It is cultivating a
steady awareness and not forgetting where we are,
what we are doing and who we are with.

Mindfulness always arises in the context of
a relationship with ourselves,
with others or with things.

Mindfulness is relaxing in the present moment and
being with what is. Mindfulness is also remembering our
inherent wisdom and responding skillfully.

Mindfulness remedies our attitude of resistance,
rejection or destruction. A condemning mind leads
to aversive states of rage, hatred, anger,
ill-will, animosity, annoyance, irritation and fear.

Subtle states of aversion include sorrow, sadness
and grief. All the various states of aversion are
conditioned reactions to what we find unpleasant.

———

When I am mindful, my body is relaxed and open
and my mind is aware and alert.

When my mind rests in the present moment
without desire for something to be different,
I am practicing mindfulness.

Investigation

DHAMMAVICAYA

*Investigation alleviates doubt or
a distracted state of mind*

Investigation is interest combined with
discriminating wisdom. It is like a flashlight that
illuminates reality. It reveals the nature of
experience and phenomena.

When we see clearly, we have perspective and know
if we are moving in a useful direction or not.

Through investigation we know when to act,
when to rest and how to balance the practice.
Investigation allows discernment between what is skillful
and non-skillful. Investigation is not an intellectual
pursuit or working to figure things out.

Investigation is used to look at emotions that might
feed aversive mind states like feelings of hurt
or self-righteousness. Sometimes fear is underneath
anger and feeding it. Becoming mindful of the
feelings often unlocks patterns. Investigation is also
discrimination of wholesome and unwholesome mental states.

———

I trust the process and practice of investigation
to reveal what is happening in this moment and the next.

When I find myself at a crossroads, I recognize that
there is no need to solve it or figure things out.
I can rest in the unknown.

Energy

VIRIYA

Energy protects one from complacency,
fear and discouragement
Antidote to procrastination and distraction

Energy is reaching deep inside ourselves and
reconnecting with our highest purpose again and again.

Energy is aroused when we maintain interest, whether it be
interest in our breath or the parade of life as it marches by.

Energy is an antidote to despair; it strengthens our inner resolve
and the belief that we can make a difference in the world.

Energy is not straining or striving. It is balanced and appropriate,
knowing when to relax and when to move forward.

Energy is not being constantly busy; busyness is a distraction
from mindfulness and the quest towards awakening.

———

I have faith in myself and therefore
the energy to pursue my worldly and spiritual goals.

I know what needs to be done and through steady determination,
I continue on the path knowing everything is waiting for me.

When I focus my effort on serving others and
alleviating suffering, I find ease and happiness.

Joy

PITI

Joy is an antidote to doubt, complacency or tension

We can increase joy by looking for it and bringing
it into our lives, knowing we deserve to be happy
and those around us deserve to be happy.

Joy is a natural result of investigating the mind and
bringing energy to our awareness. We can incline the
mind towards joy by purposefully finding beauty in nature.

When we judge, compare or fix others or ourselves,
it blocks the quality or sense of joy.

Joy does not ignore the world of injustice, racism or poverty.
Instead, joy contributes to being present and compassionate.

Joy is realized when we are generous, serving others and
invite creativity to flow out, back, through and around us.

———

When I let go of needing to be someone or
taking myself too seriously,
I allow joy and humor to be present.

When I cultivate conditions to stay present, calm,
tranquil, and relaxed, I incline my mind towards joy.

When I shift my attention from grief
to peace for myself and others, I open to joy.

Tranquility

PASSADDHI

Tranquility is an antidote to restlessness and worry

Tranquility is the soothing factor of mind that quiets the disturbances.
It is felt as peacefulness in both the mind and the body.
With tranquility the nervous system calms down.

Tranquility is soft, effortless, and peaceful.
It is a state of not needing anything more.

Sometimes calm and tranquility may feel like boredom.
Notice when the mind reaches for something to stimulate it.

Nature can be very tranquil.

When a mind is tranquil a natural genuineness,
honesty and freedom from duplicity are present.

When I find myself in a state of excitement, agitation or distraction,
I recognize this as my mind without tranquility.

May I develop calm through relaxing and
settling into my present experience.

When my body relaxes, my mind becomes stable,
I experience tranquility.

Cultivating a calm and balanced mind,
I can find composure in the midst of difficulty.

Concentration

SAMADHI

Freedom from agitation and restlessness

Concentration is a quality of mind that is soft, still and open.
With concentration the mind is malleable and flexible.
Concentration fine-tunes all other mindfulness factors.
It builds the stability to have deeper insight
into the changing nature of things.

Concentration is also the unification of the mind. It is mental
stability and a mind without distraction. Concentration is
steadying the mind on a single object, a one-pointedness,
directed to changing objects moment to moment.

One way to develop or arouse concentration is
to become aware of when it is present and when it is not.
A practitioner may also reflect and practice ethical conduct (sila),
or reflect on this precious life.

One may strengthen concentration through
dedicated meditation practice
on long retreat and through continuous daily practice,
building stability on the breath or meditation objects.

A dedicated practitioner can experience
strong concentrated states of
loving-kindness, compassion, appreciative joy and equanimity.
In this mind state, one is free of limiting perceptions,
hostility and ill will.

With concentration the mind is prepared and open
for liberation and freedom.

Equanimity
UPEKKHA

Antidote to indifference, worry and busy mind

Equanimity describes a state of balance.
Even when things don't go as planned,
equanimity imbues the mind with a calm radiance.

Equanimity is freedom from all points of self-reference.
It is indifference only to the demands of the ego-self and
its craving for pleasure and position.
Equanimity is not indifference or unconcern for others.

An equanimous mind accepts the fact of pain in the world.
It understands that suffering and cruelty are part of this world
and it engages and responds anyway.

Equanimity is the culmination and perfection of the divine abodes
of loving-kindness, compassion and altruistic joy.

I can experience equanimity when I feel
a deep sense of letting go.

When my mind is free of the habit of grasping or pushing away,
I know I can handle whatever comes my way.

With equanimity my mind is calm and still,
unperturbed and unruffled.

Practices for Opening the Mind and Heart

Self Compassion

When I recognize my inherent discontent or the wish
for something to be different, I say to myself
"this is suffering" and I treat this notion
with love and compassion.

When I feel the pain of my life, I no longer run or hide
or find avenues of avoidance. Instead, I trust my
suffering as a gateway to greater compassion.

I can connect with my own deep tenderness by
allowing myself to be with other's pain and suffering.

When I recognize my self-judging mind or victimhood
mentality, I recognize my own wounded heart.
In this moment, I find the courage to be open
and tender towards myself.

When I feel lonely and afraid, I find a way to let go of
struggling against it and turn to the compassion that
lies deep within my own heart.

In knowing my deepest suffering, I allow myself
to open to my quivering and compassionate heart.

Forgiveness
KHAMA

There are many ways that I have hurt and
harmed others, betrayed or abandoned them,
caused them suffering, knowingly or unknowingly,
out of my pain, fear, anger, and confusion.
I ask for your forgiveness.

Forgiveness to myself
There are many ways that I have hurt and
harmed myself. I have betrayed and abandoned
myself many times through thought, word,
or deed, knowingly or unknowingly.
For the ways I have hurt myself through action
or inaction, out of fear, pain, or confusion,
I now extend a full and heartfelt forgiveness.
I forgive myself.

Offering forgiveness to others
There are many ways that I have been harmed
by others, abused or abandoned, knowingly or
unknowingly, in thought, word or deed.
I now remember the many ways others have
hurt or harmed me, wounded me, out of
fear, pain, confusion, or anger.
I have carried this pain in my heart too long.
To the extent that I am ready, I offer forgiveness.
To those who have caused me harm,
I offer my forgiveness, I forgive you.

Living with Uncertainty
or Don't Know Mind

Life is chaotic, unstable, dynamic, uncertain and challenging.

We can find ways to be comfortable with not knowing what the future holds.
It takes being fully present, feeling the quivering nature of your heart and
staying with your experience without expectation or an attachment to the outcome.

Living with uncertainty takes courage.
The truth is, *everything* is uncertain, except death.

We can choose to be tossed around by the drama of our lives
and let emotions control us
or to be a spectator of the drama and tune into the energy
of the thoughts and emotions as they come and go.

When I grow anxious or afraid in the face of not knowing an answer or outcome
I interrupt my thoughts and recognize they are just that, thoughts.
I have many. It's okay not to know.

Life has moments of uneasiness and sometimes these moments seem to
last forever. Rather than running away, numbing out or being in denial,
I allow myself to be curious and lean in and ask "What's this about?"

I accept and welcome the fundamental ambiguity of this human experience
without any judgment of "this is right or this is wrong," it just is.

I let go of my resistance to the place I find myself in right now. Instead, I relax into
not knowing what's ahead, how I'm going to get out of this mess or whether or
not I have the capacity to fix anything. I just don't know, and that's okay.

When I am fearful and afraid, I let go. I can be comfortable with uncertainty.

Gratitude

KATANNU

Gratitude is a feeling or attitude of gratefulness or appreciation for
the conditions of one's life or the gifts one has received.
The more we deepen our awareness and appreciation,
the more spontaneous and profound our gratitude will be.

Gratitude is a form of openness and generosity that strengthens
relationships and eases tension, resentment and anger.

Gratitude is the wisdom of knowing that we are not independent,
we are connected to one another and through connection
we have a greater capacity to offer mutual support.

When we practice gratitude it brings delight and helps to balance
a tendency to focus on the negative or a distorted view of life.

———

I am grateful for the family, friends, teachers, benefactors,
and all those who have come before me who have made it possible
for my existence, comfort, education and safety.

Rather than focusing on what is wrong or irritating,
I focus on what is good or going well in my life.
I embody an experience of gratitude to
soften my heart and open my mind.

As I adopt a state of selfless gratitude to emerge and grow,
my mind becomes more spacious and quiet and
I consciously release fear or desire and
the idea that I need something else.

I relax and rejoice in the simple pleasures of my natural breath,
my beating heart and for this precious gift of being alive.
I am grateful for my life.

Humility

SAGARAVATA

Humility is a quality of the heart that is patient,
compassionate and authentic in its sincerity. Humility is a
willingness to hear the truth, however unpleasant it might be.

Humility is letting go of the idea that you are the center of the universe.

Being humble allows us to open and become aware of the
interconnection between all sentient beings. Humility is the attitude
of experiencing the world and everything it contains with wonder
and awe. It is about seeing ourselves as a small part of a vast cosmos,
inhabited by people and creatures from whom we can learn and grow.

Humility is freedom from ego and leads to a deep inner peace.
When we are humble, we freely express our love for
one another without any conditions
or expectations of getting something in return.

—◆—

In the spirit of humility, I have the courage and freedom to say,
"I have made a mistake," "I don't know," "I was wrong,"
"Please forgive me."

As I shift my perception from 'me' to 'other,'
I find delight in letting go of 'me.'

The decisions I make are based on deep respect for life and
humankind and what is fair and just, without regard to my image or
what others may think of me.

When I can let go of 'me' and my projections,
perceptions, fantasies, desires and aversions,
I rest easy in spaciousness and open-minded awareness.

The Eight Worldly Winds

PLEASURE AND PAIN
PRAISE AND BLAME
FAME AND DISREPUTE
GAIN AND LOSS

The eight worldly winds are pleasure and pain,
praise and blame, fame and disrepute, gain and loss.
They are pairs of opposites: One we are attracted to, the other repulsed by.
The conditions of their blowing are beyond us and can't be controlled.
When we get carried away by these winds we can easily stray off course.
Pleasure, fame, praise and gain all make us feel good.
Our ego may be bolstered by fame,
we may lose sight of our responsibilities with pleasure,
rely on external validation with praise,
or feel exceedingly comfortable with gain.
These things we all desire delude our clear minds.

———

Conversely, we can be carried away by their opposites.
We can become absorbed by our pain, our esteem can suffer from disrepute,
we can feel excessively guilty with too much blame,
and loss can leave with us with endless grief.
Being swept away by any of these eight winds causes emotional instability.
Stirring things up they cloud our clarity.
We therefore aim to set a course down the middle.
Not going directly against the wind, or with it.
We respond and accept each wind without following it,
realizing its conditions are impermanent.
Then when the wind changes direction we can respond flexibly.

Rousing Wind Horse
AWAKENING CONFIDENCE PRACTICE

*A beautiful practice to use in the morning,
or when you are 'caught' or 'hooked,' or
whenever you are afraid, or anytime at all.*

Begin with a meditation posture,
close your eyes and begin.

Allow yourself to be completely present, silently
ask "where am I right now?" Be completely
honest with yourself. You may feel good, bad, dull,
or alert. Be open to wherever you are.

Soften and open to this present experience.
Give space and warmth to whatever is happening.
You can expand your heart and mind limitlessly,
far beyond the hopes and fears of 'me.'
Far beyond the cocoon of "for me" and
"against me." Have confidence that you
can dispel your own darkness.

Open your eyes abruptly and radiate out.
Let warmth and spaciousness radiate out
to all beings and the earth itself. This is
the non-aggressive, tender hearted,
confidence in your longing heart to help others.

You are a spark of goodness, trust yourself!

Awareness of Death

The Five Recollections
UPAJJHATTHANA SUTTA

I am of the nature to age.
I have not gone beyond aging.

I am of the nature to be ill.
I have not gone beyond illness.

I am of the nature to die.
I have not gone beyond death.

All that is mine, beloved and pleasing,
will change and vanish.

I am the owner of my actions, heir to my actions,
born of my actions, related to my actions,
supported by my actions.
Whatever actions
I shall do, whether good or evil,
of that I shall be the heir.

Mindfulness of Death
MARANASSATI SUTTA

May I be open with others and myself about my dying.
May I be open to receive other's love and compassion.
May this time in my life assist me in opening my heart
to compassion for myself and for all beings.
May I forgive myself for mistakes I may have made
and things l may have left undone.
May I forgive those who are fearful of my suffering
and are uncertain as to what to say.
May all those whom I have harmed forgive me, and
may I forgive those who have harmed me.
May loving-kindness sustain all my caregivers and myself.
May I and all beings live and die peacefully.

ADAPTED AND PERSONALIZED FROM:
BEING WITH DYING BY: JOAN HALIFAX

Preparing for Death

The time has come. Death is approaching.
My body loses power, it becomes weak
as the earthly element dissolves.
Knowledge of earthly activity becomes obscure and unclear.
Images of the past, present and future
begin to merge together.
My body begins to shrink and the water element dries.
Salvia, sweat, urine and blood deteriorate.
I lose my cognitive ability to feel pleasure, pain or neutrality.
The element of fire extinguishes and I
no longer desire food or drink.
The names and affairs of those close to
me no longer have resonance.
My inhalations become weak and exhalations strong.
The wind element of movement diminishes, my physical
actions still, breath fades.
The world and my understanding of it dissolves.
My internal light sputters and becomes small.
Consciousness moves up through the central channel
of the physical body that once held me.
My heart drops, darkness spreads through the body.
There is no 'me.'
Emptiness . . . Letting go
The clear light of death is present, spaciousness abounds.
A release . . . into the mystery.
Freedom and liberation.

After Death

A Blessing for another who has gone before you

May you be free now.
May you be freed from the limitations
of the earthly mind.
May the essence of your true nature,
all that is good and pure and wholesome be released into the
infinite vast sky,
into the universal energy of the
cosmos and beyond.
May you be met by other beautiful spirits and enlightened
ones.
May you be shown the way to
unconditional love,
omniscient wisdom, boundless peace,
total joy and invincible energy.
May you be infinitely blessed,
protected and supported
on this journey into infinite bliss.
May immeasurable joy and infinite
peace surround you always.
May you be liberated.
May you be free.

Grief

Grief is one of the heart's natural responses to loss.
When we grieve we allow ourselves to feel the truth of our pain,
the measure of betrayal or tragedy in our life.
By our willingness to mourn, we slowly acknowledge, integrate,
and accept the truth of our losses.
Sometimes the best way to let go is to grieve.

It takes courage to grieve, to honor the pain we carry.
We can grieve in tears or in meditative silence, in prayer or in song.
In touching the pain of recent and long-held griefs,
we come face to face with our genuine human vulnerability.

Without a wise way to grieve, we can only soldier on, armored and unfeeling,
but our hearts cannot learn and grow from the sorrows of the past.
To meditate on grief, let yourself sit breathing into the area of your chest.
Take one hand and hold it gently on your heart.

As you continue to breathe, bring to mind the loss or pain you are grieving.
Let the story, the images, the feelings comes naturally.
Hold them gently. Take your time.
Let the feelings come layer by layer, a little at a time.
Let whatever feelings are there, pain and tears, anger and love,
fear and sorrow, come.
Touch them gently. Let them unravel out of your body and mind.
Breathe and hold it all with tenderness and compassion.
Kindness for it all, for you and for others.

The grief we carry is part of the grief of the world. Hold it gently.
Let it be honored.
Releasing the grief we carry is a long, tear-filled process.
Yet it follows the natural intelligence of the body and heart.
Trust it, trust the unfolding.

**ADAPTED FROM: "THE ART OF FORGIVENESS,
LOVINGKINDNESS, AND PEACE" BY JACK KORNFIELD**

Impermanence Chant

ANICCA VATA SANKHARA

Anicca vata sankhara
Upada va-ya dhammino
Uppajjitva nirujjhanti
Tesam vupasamo sukho

———

All things are impermanent.
They arise and they pass away.
To be in harmony with this truth
Brings great happiness.

I'm Meditating

Please Join
Me in Silence

I'm Meditating Please Join Me in Silence

BIBLIOGRAPHY AND PERMISSIONS

Buddha is as Buddha Does, by: Lama Surya Das. © 2007, HarperCollins, New York, NY.

Being with Dying: Cultivating Compassion and Fearlessness in the Presence of Death, by: Joan Halifax. © 2008, Shambhala Publications, Inc., Boulder, CO. www.shambhala.com

Lamp in the Darkness, by: Jack Kornfield. © 2014, Sounds True Inc., Boulder Colorado.

Living Beautifully with Uncertainty and Change, by: Pema Chodron. © 2012, Shambhala Publications, Inc. Boston, MA. www.shambhala.com

Mindfulness: A Practical Guide to Awakening, by: Joseph Goldstein. © 2013, Sounds True, Inc., Boulder Colorado.

The Mind Illuminated, by: Chuladasa (John Yates, Ph.D. and Mattew Immergut, Ph.D. with Jeremy Graves). © 2015, Dharma Treasure Press.

Parami: Ways to Cross Life's Floods, by: Ajahn Sucitto. © 2012, Amaravati Publications.

Peaceful Death Joyful Rebirth, by: Tulku Thondup. © 2005, Shambhala Publications, Inc.

Practicing Wisdom: The Perfection of Shantideva's Bodhisattva Way, by: His Holiness the Dalai Lama. Translated and edited by: Thupten Jinpa. © 2004 Tenzin Gyatso.

SPECIAL THANKS TO:

My husband Michael, who labored over this work as much as I did and worked as an excellent proofreader! My beautiful daughter Alexandra Lyon, who has provided me with many opportunities to practice what lies within these teachings.

ADDITIONAL THANKS TO:

Marcia Craighead, Adrianne Ross, Karen Wilson, Arlene Doris, Trudy Goodman, Philip Moffitt, Ann Cushman, Patti Breitman and Mark Rabkin.

ABOUT ELIZABETH

Elizabeth has assumed many roles in this life including being a wife, mother, student and yoga and meditation teacher. She is a founding partner of the non-profit organization Impact Giving. Most recently she has dedicated her time to writing about her experience as she explores and embodies the wisdom of the teachings of Buddhism.

Elizabeth lives with her kind, generous and supportive husband Michael, in San Anselmo, California.

Made in the USA
San Bernardino, CA
17 June 2017